THE REAL HORSE

Camino del Sol

A Latina and Latino Literary Series

THE REAL HORSE

poems

FARID MATUK

THE UNIVERSITY OF
ARIZONA PRESS

TUCSON

The University of Arizona Press

www.uapress.arizona.edu

© 2018 by Farid Matuk

All rights reserved. Published 2018

ISBN-13: 978-0-8165-3734-1 (paper)

Cover design by Leigh McDonald

Publication of this book is made possible in part by the proceeds of a permanent endowment created with the assistance of a Challenge Grant from the National Endowment for the Humanities, a federal agency.

Library of Congress Cataloging-in-Publication Data
Names: Matuk, Farid, author.
Title: The real horse : poems / Farid Matuk.
Other titles: Camino del sol.
Description: Tucson : The University of Arizona Press, 2018. | Series: Camino del sol : a Latina and Latino literary series
Identifiers: LCCN 2017042849 | ISBN 9780816537341 (pbk. : alk. paper)
Subjects: | LCGFT: Poetry.
Classification: LCC PS3613.A8756 A6 2018 | DDC 811/.6—dc23 LC record available at https://lccn.loc.gov/2017042849

Printed in the United States of America
♾ This paper meets the requirements of ANSI/NISO Z39.48-1992 (Permanence of Paper).

الوطن عند مصر

Who should the poet's voice be for?

—Roque Dalton

For a daughter among the navigators, among the names.

CONTENTS

THE REAL HORSE

Dear daughter,

We really did sit in the playground at your school this summer listening to cicadas drone loopy and sly. In my head they sounded like professionals narrating their work into online performance reviews, like lovers or sex workers narrating their sex into phone cameras. Out loud we wondered if their noise might fold the distance in the background into something that would reach us.

I don't know when you'll read this, but I started these poems as a way to see you even before you arrived, anxious about how the body we gave you would bear power's projections. I'm simple, so it took me a long time to recognize the circle I was making. I thought I could write something you could use, but you already resist the orders, displacing generation from genealogy, paternity from ownership.

Otherwise, I'm just trying to keep up with your natural-born solutions to the problem called space that here is said to come large and without mercy. This "first world" would be valued for counting us — patriated or natural-born — among its circumstantial few. You show me that even if the outlines of our circumstance burn without consequence, we can tend at once to the plain moment and to material things and to the projections they bear.

Someone is always poised to compare that tending to the cicadas' hum, saying it drones out reason or that it tries to fill the gap between estranged things with a self-positioning song. That's okay, because maybe our tending is already figured in a favorite book's title that says *Life in a Box is a Pretty Life*.

I mean, maybe it's on us to make it ugly, or even prettier, or to see that it's always also some other way. I don't know, but I don't think we're in the box alone or practicing the same contortions.

Some of us get out all the time, riding what?

Maybe the best thing to do outside is litter the panorama, interrupting the idea of roaming an expanse without end.

I've been reading about performance artist Tehching Hsieh; he was undocumented in the 1980s, like me. I was the age you are now when Hsieh came to this country to braid art into life by committing to the frame of the made thing. In that frame, when he tried to get free, he went into a cage. When he escaped time, he punched a clock on the hour. When he spoke, he made sure a friend sealed the tapes that recorded his words.

You and Hsieh make me wonder if freedom might be neither public nor private, if what sometimes gets called the aesthetic might be happiest at war not with material things but with the anesthetic.

Where does opposition go after it frames our beautiful camaraderie? I'm learning from you that we can stay, unrushed in our figuring.

Where these poems are something like sonnets, I'm trying to draw the box a song makes in the air, a box into which we can turn away. Maybe that's a space where we come together as one another's occasions, not in relation, but in service with a little ♪, in service to the little things you say to twist or wipe away the track of the next minute.

Inside, I took out what punctuation I could to make more room for you.

Your Instructions

you are somebody else

who didn't know me ever

pretend that but I was going

to be here next to you and the horse

walked between us really

slow but really and then a fire came

and didn't hurt anybody

but only the horse forgot about it

then I'll tell you what the words said

the shadow was a plane pretend that

when you take your face out of the water

but then you have to take the water out of the bowl

with you like that dream I only ever had two dreams

but then I was at Pump It Up with all my friends

A Daughter Having Been of the Type

Popular in the eighteenth century across Spain's viceroyalties, sets of *casta* paintings rendered in each panel a mother, father, and child with a caption that labeled the type such breeding vectored: *De mestizo e India, nace coyote. De indio y cambuja, nace lobo torna atrás.*

Popular in California through the second half of the nineteenth century, studio and field photographs (taken in Sacramento, unspecified, Los Angeles, Bodie, unspecified . . .) documented those condemned within and without the law. Mounted on card stock, they were sold or traded as keepsakes.

In 1857 Juan Flores and his men killed Sheriff James Barton and most of his posse in the hills outside Los Angeles. The accusation that "La Chola" Martina Espinoza tampered with the Barton posse's guns moved landed white and Californio men together to lynch poor brown men. The only known photograph of Espinoza, a street portrait, was taken late in her long life and under a bright sun.

having been raised in friends

sailing up the river to the world so far the wrong way

a tidal bore as an actuary wave brings a girl etched at the prow

bearing shining hospitality we told her to

and do you come to learn you are following appetites we trail

through a tribe somewhere called a claim to life

if you exceed the world refusing categories

and the emancipatory projects these prescribe

we're playing a game called a game or pledge of resistance

where a boy speaks fast at the pizza stand more available to be seen

the young in their concerns amid the old artifice nonstop

letting go the signs thrown up above their heads along the West Coast

liquid kids displayed right at the edge of a voice

comes a fold careless of time bearing everything besides

having ordered our faces into types by the planes

water cuts into stones or by furloughed light

that visits purpling the sheer sides of Cascadia

Saddleback Cordillera Andes Jabal Bahra

light that visits animals sleeping fearless

and afeared our grain of fur

in outlines laid at the fingertips of settlers

indolence they said having issued from a mestizo

in names in love with an Indian hardly capable

of managing a territory or a coyote's face

pushed into form aside property

by how many degrees and of what

how could this be about freedom

that a coyote go turn in its type

a daughter Juan Flores curled onto my chest

a daughter plein air

a mother archive erasure

a daughter durable good durable history
a daughter over the throwing

a father blacken the hills

a father high and tight
a father reservoir of poses

good foot
sure shot glory sign without doubt

greaser horse thief
albumen print

a daughter handle their guns

gelatin silver print

                              preformatted postcard paper

running blurry pink mouth

                         a mother commercial surf pop echo

a daughter shout pouch
a father rendered by or under the inspection of

                              mestizo castizo coyote lobo versino

a mother waste not want

                         a region of objects

photo plate 12

                         a daughter sell the shadow
                         caddisflies

a daughter unblushing

a mother rhyolite

a daughter turn away the night

a daughter her own sex

a daughter her fumbling
a daughter mission

delay the form

courtesy of

a mother not a lane

a father the empty highways

the farms to market

a daughter tucked under my chin
a daughter watching streetlights

carte de visite

funny name

a mother thirty-thousand-foot view

panorama nostalgia ghost

mineral depression

a daughter vitamin free

a father crystal mane

a mother amber leaf light

a father hole within the hole

a daughter twelve-sail cruiser

or we could go mirrored upon the face of the waters that bear loose slide surfboards

shaped for this break or upon the plains where winds arrange those who aspire to a safe room

those who fall off the beat those who fall off the sad feeling in the story of Ellington

arranging a confidence from your ear like believe we were good having gone this far from Peru

from my dad beating her into foreign reaches my mother with her sisters cleared

refugees from the country of women cruising with our bad taste inside we were illegal

on paper then say we were a patriated glory borne faster upon the face of the waters

checking our miracles against the stories of a usable past going off in drunk songs

in right-to-work uniforms exponentially articulated going all around even in the English sound

of the names brought on us dick-nosed bearded swill buckets we were what shouldn't matter

to you now already gone the lantana generating at your feet so proud rightly of your chaos

of your trumpets chambered in carports gilding the day's region of objects

but will you come to say for yourself   as some say as a sign and claim to getting over

in an echoing true name something like I am an American artist and still the question may come   did the landed come to your mothers' beds

masked in the busy snouts of animals   or were they born that way

do you get to follow them back

say it's not like that   it gets kinda rough

on the back of the horse   in the back of our limousine sailing

as real across a sea why wouldn't we expect another desert

out the windshield quinoa amber light fronds wave up the hill and back

up dancers raise stockinged knees to the left   describe the world

new romantics sing precisely of women and pictures inside me

our grown heads against the glass like Saint Sebastians

displayed under a moon that petrifies we went loping snout free

fuzzed out the night the Pacific   went louder

every tree a channel to talk in eucalyptus peels

that lined the road in eucalyptus oil unblushing at wildfire

and salt blew back an orange was feeding you   reaching up peppermint

tea fog against your mother's ribs against the door hung

so possible   now your long feet walk a new topography down the lane

run to catch up   fog turn away the night

night turn away the moon

moon turn away so we can see it

lamp in the night could be a name for each Syrian hill poised along my mother's line

now burning   and my landed greed's love wishes you   a right to rest in any country's dust

no matter the habits or confusions or what jellyfish   washed ashore might think of you

       animal

       oyster

       roe

       beef

wrapped in a warm feeling fearing you   the prophet in his glory needed to know

what a people said about him outside   still water and doe piss and reed straws

sucking the lagoon up inside themselves to share in life   a people says

sprinkle the unused words to the bottom   a people says we are as good

as each feather tip of brush grass reaching into the wind   this coast is exploding

all over the waves leaves are hungry I can tell you about it   I'm trying to not forget

the lyric part the noise you'll welcome as a twin the faster cymbals ringing

all down the hill   the ocean swills in from the south one wave by the arch rock

the next on its shoulder and so on to the point   the point lifts them up

there are holy women   somewhere alive with your techne with your name

Mary meant "of the sea" even if pictures don't hold anyone still cement pipe cover painted blue shattered peels of blue paint in the grass

and Andean hills seemed quiet forever   should we call our names to a moon gone slicing

a meter from the mountain that left my dad trying to be a dad by owning us

that left him rendered by or under the inspection of colonial art academies reaching

through generations in lightfast oil paints   do I let what can leave the house as a type

called "Cheese of all the milks"   "Suspended in midair" or "Taking a step back"

from whiteness going low three coyotes hump down the valley deep in peeled exteriors

in the hay dust come to see scrub brush scents the path of what fire will be called

alongside a shoulder   remembers itself from its impressions   newly in the photographs

I look for local kill sites   Sacramento then unspecified then us   sweat

straw smell   heavy stage curtains not what was said in the nose   or on the good foot

everything is leaving   upon the face of the waters gone so far into a next name

if we're fish baskets when caulked with sedge   caddisflies   sweet flag

            are we called winnowing sieves when hauled across land

I mean friends and local ghosts could pass through us

they want to see yellow flowers in the desert
and boys on their dirt bikes going in saturated shadows

and light-sensitive paper solutions invite allegory at every turn

like if you're walking any of your faces at the encounter into paper
emulsified for pictures in silver salts or bitumen it's at least 1841

when settlers would minister a seduction pressing you into silver nitrate
along a vast sheet can you see your hand   in the sky behaving itself
each wrinkle on the paper claimed into a new type

table salt to silver nitrate making a sensitivity to light
gelatin in iron salts the cyanotype calotype platinotype

in pigment gum arabic with potassium dichromate oil

and bromoil prints will you be closer to the falling away
of the gaze of things choosing the process

a daughter Juan Flores   or a real outlaw daughter

curled onto my chest looking doubled   exactly like us

does it matter our decorations can't help themselves

stepping out ahead in a horizon line's bands of purple black

every night stacked on this unlit town over young heads

crowded by a bubbling upsweep into something like a curio

from each glass nook watch what friendly air may come   borrowing Flores's eyes

said to be "neither black gray nor blue greatly resembling those of the owl"

listen for chaste nouns in time   some mercury   silver   mylar

little verbs   if any   "that were ever set in a human head"

transactions being forms that change what's to see

not how to move through the mirrored rooms of the dead restored

to a fresh churned smell   after my hand stained with outside worries an inner wall

no collapse   a turning over greed for the picture archive I lose my place

but stamped on the tin frame of our mirror
two long-tailed birds kiss a flower between them

it's like some people you see

proud with their daytime running lamps and metals in the sun   a posse

can think it comes home to flashing eyes of señoritas they say   little lady lords

out West   a land dotted with practitioners full of old commercial surf pop echo

that wants nothing but projection   seas   awesome trees

in the wind archive wanting the voice-over   the sun ghost   Los Angeles a clean

way to hug the young   ocean salt on desert air ghosts the cool

expanse of the hour ahead   we'd try not to show our eyes until they passed

bright white light these days better than a day searching eyes could so easily interrupt

at least you're in it   is that the success   when trees shake over sisters

or brother trees make shadow pools for drone traffic the record doesn't say

Sheriff Barton's posse was a white as cute as eye shadow as a model plane the men

take to the quiet depth so well dead they said cuz "La Chola" mishandled their guns

Boeing Phantom Ray shadows the record in its truth and beauty kinsmen

go down nattering   stir the bowl into a reservoir   moon   little one   our water if there's already an archive in the noise where you're the outlaw

we'll bring you messages in the willows   in the citrus fields

high bright flowers reek a spice for free   and if the sheriff drops his big voice

on Sepulveda making a show   out of being a thing   with you when the cymbals go

echoing in the finger bells   sibilant into the fan   sways the hills

at his yellow heels   when he asks about the desperate

like it's not everyone's name   says it was your fault   that Predator

engine hum always stored under the stairs   so what if you signaled your men

with a lit cigarette in a house by night   we could still play in the sunshine

all orange marker we'll draw a box seen from above keep decorating it

with stickers Christmas-themed presents and glittering Christmas-eyed

mermaids is what a people are saying about him

no history no   figuring no I mean really

if we could gather thick as these stickers about him

never suiting what we make   to a commons that needs a "shout pouch" fashioned

from "a fact of a most beautiful necklace of human ears on a rawhide string"

even if your names open beneath you intimate as your next thought cymbaling

on the shore arranging all those grains of sand   mica in the mosaic of the bank portico

what lived and storied coordinates   that you're young   that you won't be blank for me

or for the cluster of antennae the remaining Barton men make of themselves

listening between understandings along the yellow fire hills of California just one

surfeit ridge could tin the wind out   ringing for the ears of the twenty

arrested since the sheriff's killing left alive in custody   and I had the nerve to look

at pictures   when buildings echo one another across the office park

draw doors on everyone   a sound can break space or enfold it   cut through the sea

as a twelve-sail clipper I said   or be the sea to eel virus and gaze   swirl the reservoir

of what was said   our shoulders remember themselves from whose impressions

grass then air   then Coloma then San Diego then unspecified sweat   straw smell   heavy stage curtains not what was said

in the nose or the good foot settles on the plastic bits cheap pretty bright red beads

loosed this wind rolls the dead   lean into a parade above our roof carry a disaster

this way   unspecified   Los Angeles   Bodie   unspecified   Shasta

toward my stepping off the strain of new thought if one day we'll be in a state   in a lost place

in a tent city will you be left to talk for us   will you see the tree of yellow flowers

the vinyl sheet pitched for a roof   water in gasoline cans hurried across hands

but today along our row of cubicles a sun staff in the blue recycle bin shows its walls

as a slight blue coalescent plastic   place a horse's jawbone   on our piles give something

to the nuns to hold   have them weave your sheets then burn us

indiscrete with your words   but for now do I keep telling you

it's not that easy to step off the dock   manic babies in sulfur and mercury in stars coming

      for us let artists be curious

      let them be alive in work

A Daughter the Real Horse

In 1861 Adah Menken started her long run playing the "breeches role" of the Cossack hero, Ivan Mazeppa. Navigating the theater houses of the United States and Europe, she used the press to alternately circulate and repudiate rumors of her mixed European and African ancestry. Each night on stage she covered her skin, though not her shape, in a pinkish white body stocking to play the culminating scene in which Mazeppa is stripped nude and bound, against a scrolling panorama, to a runaway horse.

what's my work
what I thought our shadow

on the distaff side
lined out women gone out
either way from you

pulling thread out of flax from the staff
writing
anything we want
depilating
or setting hair

if each dimension in time is also another
already folded in or stacked on top

our work might fall off the display
but maybe we don't

during the war being a reliable thing to say

        what metals went into the sentence

        into the tack and spurs if iron was cheap

let's say iron with what vigilance the books say

        was in the air

        everyone came to see the rebel

hero sent away in Adah's body

        a thing she mastered onstage

        until it was a room she could leave

            shavings of metal on her fingertips

animal grease   in her teeth in her century

           no edits or quick takes outside of a train

or strapped to a horse   onto that externalizing love

        machines call up

like when it rains

drops shine slow in our desert

air threaded

about the water tower

and eucalyptus grove

like stage curtains

heavy until they're not

like any of the videos that assume one day

you'll join those of us still looking

the curtains lighten

but never fall off the little swarms

Napoleon Sarony's publicity pictures

lifted and split Adah into

"a New Orleans baby"

"I will create a new sensation   depend on it"   Adah promised

that shudder in a long sequence where sides fold in time

in edits in the eye she put herself there and gone

in a dummy's place tied to a real horse

riding four stories up a narrow ramp a new feeling

off a great horsewoman   wolves on the run Inca doves fog the stage   for an ideal man

of refinement taciturn was a woman seen   in their thousands

conical retina tunnels layering   each other's looking so many times

did it feel like they slapped space red to its surface   then a fine

ash in the wrinkles   it's not a space for details that fall away in words

clean blood   where no one steps in the reservoir you can see it between us

seeping in degrees crusting or draining   into various attitudes rendering

feelings her busy arms would strip the air

clean of critics saying   "She poses better than she speaks"

what of it reaches home   hot wax pulling my mother's hairs   leaving her
made smooth where she made herself white   having looked   like a man

at her   I could be one more thing   shared across the light "artifactual"   anything could be a mirror coupling

the stripped robes was a shining copper flower clip   in the aspect of a nipple

the Cossack hero didn't care   in the work of raising her shield

in her hair in the shine of her toes   dipped in oils from the dark horse hide

are we a successful people   putting your wilderness

in the wide eye of the horse for you   imagine the smallness of a European room

beyond stylized tendrils of whipping mane as long as we're looking   the mirror

was supposed to pass for our eyes   my daughter Glaucon the negations

were supposed to open as gates   an immigrant California baby like me   or a local

made white enough to not begin exposed   had to first pale beside someone like Laulerack

Adah's "Indian maiden"   then beside "the African beauty" French producers

threatened to cast   then beside the horse's shine   we were supposed to fold edges

to look full on into an expanse of edges

where our trot could achieve   whose particular   speed the horse might say engorged my tongue escapes its mouth but in sympathy

the world will increase a color on the walls

the backs of your knees open to drink in

or maybe the horse would say there never is a stage

much less the sand in which the theater sinks

there is the dove and its shadow over the hero and her horse

and the shadow is dense with its turning iterations

and wet with its water and light with their light

so if we have to realize generations

of recorded advice like "Go find some spectacle

where your pretty face will show"

we can try it on loop   and when the metals

go loose of their tape

they can light out for the Territory

"a vagabond of fancy"

"the interest is painful in its intensity"

"When the animal   affrighted by the glare of fires and goaded"

"the trail winding up between jagged rocks"

"above a roaring stream to vanish on heights unguessed"

"Born a dweller in tents   a reveler in the tented habitation of war"
the whole country gorgeously illuminated

say it's not your shame because it's our shame
or we're left available   that's us
blue sky behaving itself and two long-tailed birds

on the frame of our mirror   draw sugar refined from a flower between them

the horse and the high ramp are givens

to both cold and warm lighting schemes we bathe across the rooms we document
by video some of us came here to be the real rider

or the real horse the real hero whose real white skin
picks up dirt water can wash and return to the ground floor of the purpling valley

"terrific cataracts   tearful precipices"   work to be a given
in the folding   if I could be one of the rooms

you pass through on your way out of you

but how do I pull from that proposition   a place for you to turn in regard

if in the story of a thing I say there was a place
it's because the placed look back

on us with this feeling face I've been reading
we could match to a green aspect in Kathakali's color-coded

system of theater where actors younger than you
learn a closed set of precisest faces and feelings

something like Adah learned hers   so what finite resistances
of mountain planes   did we make in your face

we came here holding on to a stake in artifice
          Emily's butterflies
plashless in the coined word   swarm close

then settle   articulating the glam out of our echo   would you

even want to run as fast   as a high-end line we could trust spinning the against movement equine of blur a..."

"...lights flashing and panorama painted of drum

what does my pale sister want thy pale sister is named Adah laid soft upon your breast Adah

would write we'll be concubines the maiden Laulerack explained where dust on the floor lifted

on a breeze broken off its current upon the stand of eucalyptus outlines where their bodies

were they filled with grayed leaves vertigo Adah would write what word there was to be said

when the eyes of a dove led her to a clearing having darkened so many sidewalks animals

get tired but dirt sparks in the traveling or I just want to be around you I just want to see us

bound folds sumptuous in exposed skin hose white legs her on feet pretty hero's A

.outline own its into running horse real this of back the on freight as

in a pool she'd write opportune your pale sister called to a party of white men a white woman

is in danger so they were flushed toward soldiers ahead of startled men in the chief's party

who pierced Laulerack letting her fall upon Adah already in the wagon Adah would write I

settled her dark curls touch she would say to white journalists who would write of the channel

on Adah's thigh where a tomahawk grazed her while your dad banged at that door in the song

I was wearing your colors to California coming to consciousness all heroines said where am I

so consequently did I come to love them for twinning me while important reviewers amateur

face sitters perch so far aside whiteness I can't even believe in the theorizing we offer them like reaching running toward and alighting from extraordinary points in sound and space

creates new pathways to a future for sophisticates who decipher semantic crosscurrents

of despair and a brief tearing at the veil of racial division makes a frontier where desire

is improvised through and across coursing histotextuality a method marginalized writers

use to braid historical allusions that contextualize and radicalize their work by countering

the putatively innocuous generic codes they seem to have endorsed a site of self making

for bodies in the cultural imaginary singing an anthem of simultaneity in a continuous space

of renewal that repeats dissonance and lack of closure as a strategy of performative

rigorously oppositional identity production a predicament bodies find themselves in

whose momentary solutions we call dance imitating with a vengeance calling attention to

the masquerade against the progressive ideology of the panorama who'll ride into a future

slipping into and out of the white parts of men trying to save women and the world putatively

bound folds sumptuous in exposed skin hose white legs her on feet pretty hero's A

.outline own its into running horse real this of back the on freight as

exposed to meet the lubricious demands of the male spectator and yet always confoundingly

and performatively surplus negotiating and traversing astride the very moment of exposure

I would sit naked and would write and by my means I would sit to write and would leave
my shoes open near the window given to its wasteful passing knowing the tugging at my door
was the wind pushing out as I would stage it flying into dissolution and that if the bigger house
came next I'd have our man bring the car around stripped of badges murdered out in fields
pima desert cotton chorusing a comfort of brotherhood sans sisterhood or brotherable things
still the background would roll past the windshield interrupted by gracious marks migrating
under no discernable hand I would step into the stall built up around the toilet I would

bound folds sumptuous in exposed skin hose white legs her on feet pretty hero's A
.outline own its into running horse real this of back the on freight as

take the porcelain figurine attitude of the feminized masculine or the masculinized feminine
punch line of my given type sitting on the toilet where there is no toilet reading the superficial
estimations on holidays I would open a panel on my back to receive the carbon powder
packed tight by a special implement and upon a flame turning at the long end of a safety match
I would burn the powder inside with a share of flux drawing its impurities ashing it in reams
of dense rope from my porcelain hole for those still looking and I would know by my intuition
rope would collect in a spiral rising on this day when I would have an intuition finer by a day

when you asked where's my pink Barbie horse at the wiped counter in the kitchen is she pretty
I thought of Mr. Hands bleeding out after taking an Arabian stallion and it's not done with me
you say pink plastic in the sky in a windstorm I see livid high-gloss plastic some artist molded
as outsized pill capsules like fast medicine sparkle colors draw saliva out first as if wide eyes
were made always available letting fly the blond crystal mane into the air all down the year
the documentary said it took a friend in the scene to learn his name decorated in the stickers
that came with it so it's totally the company's fault and men's fault with appetites for a self
gone into ready eyes or for friendly sex that would put consent into the air to be increased
when our drive goes right past the horse track's delicately arched brutalist concrete we're still
in bodies we don't have to own to care for what the foreground rolling back leaves them to be

bound folds sumptuous in exposed skin hose white legs her on feet pretty hero's A
.outline own its into running horse real this of back the on freight as

if so many once straddled dirt bikes in nylon shorts thinning at grown eyes come to wrap us
in being seen who should want the freedom of seeing a toy horse and thinking Mr. Hands
come down live again with a faith in all the obviousness of form Mr. Hands you're not done so
sing Mr. Hands gonna get fucked tonight Mr. Hands gonna get fucked tonight Mr. Hands

gonna join a chorus called a tradition of saying of the horse as of the adolescent

bear in a tree in the square it's just nuisancing for a study of relative values

so when the whole afternoon's air falls into a flat white light at the classroom's

glass spur its pane rolled back from any impression straining at its lead inviting

the lame question who's walking whom that's when I most want to ask after a right

to kill the bear so later you might go shameless sensing for yourself and still judging

the pull of walking out onto a field where small European rooms Bataille or de Sade

stand their frames even if we can go there to feel just like whites with good shots

and with our own hunting guide to bend and open over the dead bear's warm fur for

and with a second guide who holds the phone taking the video to its generic failure

and the first again cheering "Shake that bear, shake that bear" claims for those of us

bound folds sumptuous in exposed skin hose white legs her on feet pretty hero's A

.outline own its into running horse real this of back the on freight as

still looking ecstasy as a mourning that substitutes animals and positions if one day

you look too you shouldn't have to abdicate a place because it's legal only means

it has a trace a small but given perch from which to assess the practice of a practice period ecstasy if we're going to stand around in the names when we could join those running

into a cousin's fields letting the contemporary fall away if the gauge is right of the nails

binding the soles to the leather I like the enamels and glazes the animals get painted in

flight as much as the animals and if you're of critical importance to some vision of the future

know nobody wants to play the North but it's not like they're not trying to win farbee farb

far be it from them to criticize but they don't invite spectators to the books telling you

what you just walked out of is history in all time rushing isn't the call but it sends you

bound folds sumptuous in exposed skin hose white legs her on feet pretty hero's A

.outline own its into running horse real this of back the on freight as

summarized at the inside of a snout mask playing pretend along the reservoir's tourist edge

where we take our walk successful neoclassical sculpture comes to poses plastique

powdering live bodies naked white or in body stockings white to look like Parian

porcelain so we could look on something like Gibson's *Tinted Venus* and see realism

itself running if the unprofessional form moved a whiteness enough to get to be a border

on the other side take the grown looking and staging for a gauge of how some would bear

staying discreet in a body as a magic in whiteness they'll say you want your share in the lay of the scrub grass I see wind's circuitry amateur videos having run in my pocket

documenting a scene is the name of the next song if expanding beyond dyads into a finite set

hardly shames the looking or the scurrying in the scrub grown folks hear as a mouse or a pair

of long-tailed birds in those positions when their noise is most in the shape of their outlines

feeling so low in our asymptomatic infections gone unmanaged by the agencies so base

gooning our grown faces so hard at the low words they spoke back to us in waves on noise

eyes on wide and say come what may inside the box or under its pall written asunder I mean

we know everything standing beside what bright and nimble forms to have been of the class

bound folds sumptuous in exposed skin hose white legs her on feet pretty hero's A

.outline own its into running horse real this of back the on freight as

that was the happiest among our types to have been raised to have thought a condition

might lay out to an edge to have fit our legs into jeans and our bellies into shirts and our

wrists into watches to forget the things we did to invite the wind through the house

and now say the ghost tugs at our door to have been called a bitch just cuz we kissed

the white noise from a line of navigators   frenzied things   to have set an aim for our eyes

to have drifted to have been possible in a flattening of relations so they lay for your regard they were little things in demands and performance reviews we did to make wall and sky sway

bound folds sumptuous in exposed skin hose white legs her on feet pretty hero's A

.outline own its into running horse real this of back the on freight as

about you as something that wasn't continuous   fair intellect lunging so fast at ugly certainties

A Daughter That She May Touch the Deployments

Among the air assets housed at the local Air Force base are eighty-three A-10C ground attack planes, fourteen EC-130 Airborne Battlefield Command and Control Center planes, five HC-130J personnel recovery carrier planes, and a contingent of F-16 fighter jets. As part of the United States Air Combat Command, the base maintains these planes ready for deployment.

you play at slapping us hard enough to get in trouble

I don't know what I speak this into at any of your ages

some men in particular will think to fuck you

already do "so unaccountable, so unreasonable, and what is usually

called so unnatural" is how Sojourner had to allow as an exceptional rule

what was given to her white woman owner whom you could have been

I mean we gave you your body and didn't change everything

like the general "shrugged evil of it so true and impossible to touch"

that Harmony wrote to her dad about after he died makes me think to wield

me and my types down onto my value if that presses its point into a hole

where one day you could drop words down through this house

arranged about the reading chair where we had a matron screaming

hard at her husband drunk in the street painted on a retablo

what good impressions it might make to allow nothing

and live screaming so composed when they say you're the prize

it may start to get worse when you turn nine not having anything

to do with you except you'll be in there bearing your body

a screen for pictures among historical materialists something

like I was bearing the hard dicks of passengers across my small arm

my head resting on the bus window the smell of rain from the bus stop

putting out a little ammonia but on Speedway today we can say anything

like rain smells good falling on the sign for Girls Girls Girls or that posed open lipped available tree trimmers carve through the medians

this morning big in their work calling out on what flat blue air

approaches you to be noticed what doesn't get staged on ambiguity itself

calling for a border or a hem brought round one sadness

is that you pick a dream and you are following

our daytime running lamps and metals in the sun

or you couldn't name the tree or its bird

or that one camera doesn't know about dignity

a little distance

to carry in time you come to us on any horizon in the house

zoo otters we saw in that pleasure gather a crowd oiling about each other

casually you kick my groin pinch your mother's nipple in sleep and suckle

what feeling your fingers root up into a top hat and tails to sing "Nobody

no time" if you want your voice to trill at least a little ways

under what we're supposed to be we won't waste one ripple

on that water my grown friends afford the pills they trade

to feel like this every day every night the car clean garaged

in seasons when this valley's dust repeats with what we call luck

and a light touch on the tops of trees that didn't ask to be on the same street

will you grow to stage in touch what your skin would bear in

from surface waters down into flesh edged in its lower courses

go agents that would prepossesses your form I mean even the air is thick with men bearing mirrors for men each the other's babies

pressing down with a faith in all the obviousness of form

do words arrive in flesh then flex a centimeter more

when you're older and read this at 10:13 the good news

of the morning's floor is that it's boring under the light

loosed ends to meet it sloppy or clean a thing

using itself wastes not want

even if we're bred migrants running back in generations

none of us knowing what animals cross the path to the reservoir

wondering about the gaze about your mouth

about killing us trying to draw a giraffe will your little head

return to the idea of a fish that in its hunger mouths how to be free

whether we call it free or don't and slip along the small rocks of the trail

our hands catching would smart from each impression

in our palms for some time taking up our places with us

announcing that echo off the sides of the people we've been to get here

and I don't know time is now smeared across the dove

mocking chickadee and cardinal calls all through this morning

I present myself spread over the words it matters

who does what and over their promises I got used to this country

gathering a people where we are now once a week at the park

rent a field bring some tea and all the adults would just watch the kids

so we might believe pleasure a techne for arraying ourselves

along some absolute bearing's deviating norths

we'll make a fire tomorrow

how many names could they have the eye beaters blind kids James used

I want to defend them from his program

the kids punched their little fists right into their eyes to flash a light

against the walls of their brains the poet wanting us prime

to really see us in the credit in our wallets when we visited

the nerve of the poem trying to be our blind face

we'll make a fire tomorrow you see if I just write what I know

I won't use anybody is part of the fantasy of being discreet

in a body as a claim to life maybe the kids beat their eyes

to learn "A New Rule in Algebra. Five from Three

and One remains!! or, The Three Mexican Prisoners

having but one leg between them all" suffering the sameness

arching your little body as the lines of fish swimming say anything

a one-legged three-bodied thing can still dance put its foot up

on the dais on the table stink up the halls of my legislature

can ghostwalk as you line up over the sets of potential turns you can use

the sets of possible intents your numbers of legs of glands

of gums of waters of hard edges everybody can draw says the artist

California oak fungus in the wind keep checking the hole to find the hole work and sex being funny if I look off to the side in homes in videos

where the agents try to come clean grouped cheering each other's instances

happy to meet the camera as bodies handling what they want

handling me as a young thing in their mouths in their cars

then thanks I have to go home for dinner I'd say the sidewalk

brightening out West far into space I wanted to carry that feeling

into the critique of feeling seeming to layer the white

onto protected things the Air Force transport works a little harder into the wind

making a rushing withdrawal like listening inside my first Walkman

that needed first a commons echoing my smell crowded walking

or cycling well above groundwater and so far above us

an unusual compass of voice taking the *A* above the staff and holding it

for fifteen seconds in an immodest display listening

your mother wrote "three whistles invoke a junction" where sly

or guileless crouched onto a platform singing to a street cat

the story of your soul the ghost of an Aleppo ballerina

might discover you white or is it patriated and protected enough

to not start out exposed but even with that bit

in my mouth I can't get us to an answer for Anne asking

after her operation something like under the sign of what body part

used up or cut off or flayed can a daughter finally "be unavailable"

to whatever various slants of porn light would try to share or foreclose you when all I want is to believe you've already gone off

into a next space in a ghostwalk with the dead and your friends

awake to expectant veil light or is once more the daughter

simply there that she may dance no back row lily

of color and if that's the picture there's a warning

about seeking a truth in sex's history striver's truth claiming

some share of freedom by turning and housing our symptoms

while walking through the kitchen or paying for the moonfish fillets

exactly like a blind diver diving the bubbles and the cabinetry

pulling up and the keypad and clerk rising into the flat blue sky

now curving around my blind fingertips look there are bees

at the cauliflowers look at my hands you say far above touching

the deployments but I'm stuck on saying they keep circling and so on

to the point where I want to see you less than to see you out

and if I can't I won't ask you to tell me how to stay

in the long shade your hands cast when they get to their totality

before the sun that we know sits high

and the sky behaves itself around the things we are making

the forms and their compensations and by scintillas you are too

but if saying should fails art maybe our art

is where we should stay and what we should exceed

like Alice writing   "but that's not the ending"

No Address

In 1849 collaborators helped Henry Brown ship himself out of enslavement by hiding his body in a parcel crate. In 1850 Brown launched his panorama show, *Henry Box Brown's Mirror of Slavery*, prompting Frederick Douglass to lament, "[H]ad not Henry 'Box' Brown and his friends attracted slaveholding attention to the manner of his escape, we might have had a thousand Box Browns per annum."

In 2003 U.S. citizen Rachel Corrie, volunteering with International Solidarity Movement, knelt her white body between the home of Palestinian pharmacist Samir Nasrallah and an Israel Defense Forces armored bulldozer. Despite appeals to U.S. officials and a suit brought by Corrie's family in Israeli courts, her death generated no judicial, diplomatic, or policy consequence.

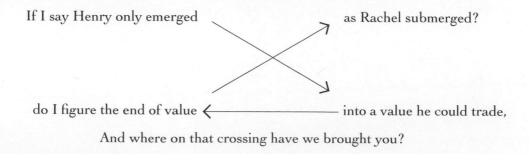

If I say Henry only emerged   as Rachel submerged?

do I figure the end of value ⟵———————— into a value he could trade,

And where on that crossing have we brought you?

Reportless Subjects, to the Quick / Continual addressed —

—Emily Dickinson

I want you to see the leaves are gone and white like winter

you said let's make like a girl mean something amazing commercial

flickered in that dead patch today is where I saw

the cardinal's glow you wanted to see me go first

to use a pleasure in seeing me   "walk behind this man" the voice said

to Duriel so she could leave the train platform alive unbarred and unafraid

feeling actual having nothing to do with little moments   the suds

in the sink lighting off workmen's calls or how some of the Buddhist advice

bends air before breaking it

birds tonight and kids thread air into each other chiasticly

it's not a word   the voice said but a pressure to impose to feel the shape you're in

tell me what to see   when you can it's a false spring after two days of rain

you splashed in little verbs   if any use us   loud without the figure like running

a voice's grain   is it a given   its facts go in boxes whose faces we etch each shave a gain moneys and birds settle by night in what formations on the reservoir lake

the roofs replaced leaves the hail brought down

flake in the sun and winds push and mound them into berms

there is no color in straw but fuel in nerves

your leg shakes and big planters hold trees

outside the stately houses around the water

I can make my bad teeth better and hang a little gold

at your wrist any verb could turn to a new feeling

waking glad to remain an owner

if whiteness or a people is a claim to life you slept through

the night in a house that stands

and our papers are filed with the state   so vacationing

we can hike up in the mountain to see the ancient pyramid

above the valley of Tepotzlán honored a tax collector

bureaucracies precede us there's a tribe somewhere we say

that trades in fear their names such a stab at beauty

we should assume they study our histories and our lyrics our gestures

and tones even if they don't exist a people's trade is fear feeling

a sudden drop of the floor when I'm far from you

and too such a picking at the earth's curved surface and all laid on it

that I'm to hold a space and from it cast the gaze you've trained in me

onto the back sides of docking bays brake places parking lots and turnabouts

and above them the sky

a bigger more respectable more competent friend

maybe an aesthetic theory like two dogs same caramel color off leashed

to chase and echo one another in the green patch

by the metro stop gold-embossed grass-threaded streets

can I be in that picture one day with you

if what etches into your eyes leaves a small canyon in its trough

is there the chattering speech

I don't think it's enough to say images   seen   the still Aleppo pine needles

a tarp billowing at the lower winds are a weather   how long could you look

in the foreground at a wet child who isn't you

the two bits of peeling white light she tossed into us feel like a skein

a weight   water falling down your back in the bath a salted

silver-edged negative pressing you to the steady light impulse

neither of us will absorb   winking in it all the while by its known waves

the state's cargo planes keep from folding into our street

having lost a few peoples running in superfluity the sky behaves itself

over bamboo that grows here wild or bedded   with river stones hauled

come to rest their smoothing ends but not the infinitive daughter

gone to running away with water as one of her rhymes

hands on the water you call scene-setting hands on the table

water over the houses and hills swimming paint a picture of a boat

put everyone's names in it all yourn standing up tall as your favorite bamboo

in the yard tell me again its leaves fold back historically materially green

over its pale shoots opening and dividing a day into rooms collected

in the picture encyclopedia any guest could see youth's decades in montaged

trunk and bikini cuts all the soft blind fingers at the walls of a day

just a day folds back to look on you like an anchor serving its subjects

floating out on a water I couldn't feel soaking into this valley of gravel

and clay five thousand feet thick under alluvial fans of boulder debris

across desert floors young volcanism made the rhyolite red that pulls the eye

into the core of mountain silhouettes   "We see shadows of people" said drone pilots

"and we kill those shadows." "That's a kid there to the left." "That's what they were calling

the adolescent earlier." "Yeah, adolescents don't move like that."

walking into a room with sadness made crystal touches me on the thigh in a brotherly way

I already know quickening flashes of teeth as people affirming a homeland are about to cum

but at any age you can tell your architect what color glass for the office park

low clouds reflected advance into their next sky next weather

let's say our right to pleasure is a withholding

as a president lies in state do you wake in state as a medium screaming

I carry no one in my eyes   not even a lane

I don't know to where you can stretch your finitude a little

I can be your thing you scream you want in your night terror to bite my mouth

"Right side up with care" *Henry "Box" Brown's*

Mirror of Slavery panorama show interrupted whose idea of escape

the magisterial fields of the horse run   dotting the rolling hills   with char with effects

with bodies used for a whiteness   from which Marina Abramović's heroics

would further empty out with a voiding majesty I don't trust   Henry's fields give the lie to a tribe somewhere saying fear because it feeds

the gull by night wheels round its technology for falling

such a handling stuns the thing isn't gentle to its otherness

be thou gentle to your animal

our finest sculptors charged with shaping a woman

Guanshiyin in her deified name means "observing the sounds of the world"

glaze her hand and leave it loose to turn or withhold

and call it a figure for compassion

the sun comes up through the planted trees a thing wastes not want

what will you in your time do with a white enough woman's form

will its light make a word in the room so un-American in its humors

and hugging near death   that we'll try to say it's not a real word either

so our anger might be civilian and yours

trying to outpace likenesses who sells the shadow

to dance only among spirit rappers in bodies where "women, negroes, natives"

it was said were acted out for Reverend Mattison they were "vehicles of impurity"

"my children too have learned a barbarous tongue, though it's not so sure

they will rise to high command" wrote Tu Fu or Bernadette on New England

a boy tried to hang a dog in a playground she said you tried several spaces today

under a desk a nook bent to your body brought round

what about all the rooms the sky makes a faint blue expanse

a long far line of electric poles a mountain I can see dog yelps almost digital

maybe from inside a car parked at the Dollar General I guess anyone dreaming a state

could visit and detonate insourcing a kind of defense   but the sky behaves itself

with just enough war over us   as a family feast photographed frames time in our house

you made your first marks today on this page

                to my empowered friends

                I love your story

like the shapes we made in the things we said were demanding of us

now you ask me why the sky is a tank full of lemonade out back

all wet tonight and bugs call up a swamp in this desert in my story

my dad wrote all the wrong names for her on a brick that could lift

through my mother's window came the words arrayed in glass

dusting San Martincito on her dresser cast in plastic with spaces in his robes

a home for the hen the dog made mild in the skirts of the mongrel saint

still lining a thin easy silence around me come the scenes all down our street

in someone's car music each word lifted into its own space thumps in the moon's

heavy sleep breath there are extensions we can read what we said

it's such a simple printshop so mothers might tell us about what came

to be more known   a pear tree in the commons and really

the words left idle beside   if they could tell us about the forms

if these came to lift them if we could ask *sin miedo y sin piedad* wouldn't they never say there was a time   what hovers turns behind maybe two feet up

from our scapulae a moon's heavy heel in the water an Aleppo daughter in my line ordered

from a bride book bringing the wrong language to the Andes her new stepkids

taking her first stillborn by the heel far from her Arabic taunting   I've seen their pictures

they were beautiful young people in those minutes did they feel in their mouths

there are spaces for the refusals but we've heard migrants carried cultures in their dough

little strains of living stretching back to outleap our generations with their own

collapsing days into what they've written for us socializing the mother function

a daughter in your mother's line grew to offer her Englishless milk to strange babies

in a Newark tenement and once in the parking lot around an igneous intrusion

we saw a daughter searching the asphalt and her father screaming "If you lost it

I will destroy you" not unhinged but large stretching the wet outlines of his organs

to chamber the particular grain of his voice's promise   and here goes my voice

trying to fit opposite promises   in relation   for you would there be no address if I try to tell it back to you what voice runs over gravel in the sentence

taking shapes on the gravel in the sentence   a dead girl given to the likeness

of a depilated face made white enough or having hired hands to shape in their skill

or having bred some not overwhelmingly disposable features having been raised

in friends' congregations in unaffected elegance taking a pledge of resistance

to kneel with International Solidarity into the stamp of that human shield

before someone else's house besieged bearing shining hospitality we told you to

give your money to the poor kneeling before a partner state's bulldozer working

a little harder into contested ground happens to flay the white from Rachel's body

how do I mark the strata of attended things descended past where I let myself be

buoyant wanting nothing more just than to be traded   it's not the dusted hurt

already layered on what Trojan baby girl would bear me out of the future pre-Rome

but wanting a fraying of the lines ridden by a claim to life as a condition so we could play

only means in my hands those lines extend   it's no better   wanting it in a doting way just smile already I know into the sunny

grainy pear rising onto my teeth it's like

some people you see by the heel

purpling held into the screen

in my pocket a position I would say

if sound was finding forms

stand in for us I hold the baby thing

pretend I didn't know you ever and say the wrong

far words all around gild the air heel in hand

in the light going through its orange

and pink turning rhinestones in the story

sustains delay to let the familiar back

at once for you which pieces won't we shed

peopleless   who says what's kin

who doubts cicada songs extend each silver green

bamboo into a whole firm canopy

who doubts the prophet groaned in the spirit's self same

sure shot glory raising Lazarus out of the mountain

box into something real   if I'm to believe my emergency

giving the type away to typos Henry emerged

on loop   are you being seen in some old eyes

with care is how some headaches need to start "Embracing, the dumb

will speak, the lame will walk!" in such promises in so much

insistence there was this César all woke drunk up in some

white people's republic rousing volunteers into freedom

bring me my horse my love my gold green pear

our general strike my gun whenever you read this what diminishment

will you know making words seem mostly signals of their own restraint

I guess yelling at you to survive doesn't change the object you are

everywhere stealing my shit   figuring and giving out rights-of-way

through me like if parenting is a thing are you childing us who gave you a face

and if César was only right where bodies have to coalesce

in great numbers before the state hails with its infrasound rays

that don't cut off the ear but shake the cochlear fluid bringing faces

onto paving stones or with rays that would excite water and fat

so the burning skin symptom can insistently affect one area or shift

the burning skin symptom can come and go rarely frequently or persist

then is that why some of us like to take pictures of so many serial things warehoused

or on docks waiting or we like to name the bougainvillea flowers

to linger in a timeless way we thought to crown you with possibility

and there isn't a day I don't hear a little circle of war storied out so I can eat it

on an oval orbit you say so even if I'm not before you alone isn't a thing

"& someone who does not love you cannot name you right" — Aracelis Girmay

like when my mother died women she worked with tending the old brought girls to chant

out of the chapel's bright plain walls a novena singing nine days into one niche

on a string their voice ran out of their voice and their voice caught up

with words they made a handling and it's right to worry about losing oneself

to a stylized rank but I don't think that's it if we're ready to fold unalone

into a voice the dead can leave love having been a casual service

casually volute   mold and casting to one another in your childing way

don't imitate my slogans in some fidelity to our line I won't rise forever maybe

I'll be near you a while thinking I need your breath to work for me where vague life

means even your blur claimed into a commons what Henry

would discontinue at each object a self same region of objects renders Israel onto Israel

California onto us   impelled toward us impediment   and back on the edge

surface of our contact turns out

a type of porcelain for casual curates   and a type of porcelain for court

"Form — it's because there are consequences." — Lisa Robertson and if words alone are tracers in the negative

I'll keep writing you   to move it welcomed

by the outline where you   could drop the word

you know you say   that's not even the most brittle shape above us

leaves are turning their gray sunless sides every which way

so to wipe gone the track of your next minute your little voice says

the reservoir goes on forever and it does   in a funny wave

shining cityscapes of gravel poised at our heads looped   a kind

delay of form of any   owned will chafed down to red silt and feeling

laid out on this dusty plain opening under a mirroring sky

its available dead look down to each grain of sand those sharpest edges

their binding single selves in facets   in such futures   to be simple and done

sparklers branch into three or four twigs at their ends every time

and in a turning over of paper   or in lacquered thinnest layers of my habits

you say you hear gold leaf   a glaze drying on the hand and honey in the mix

each the other's animals we keep talking to move the words is a sounding

so if the dead and the shipped get to us   we could be not a people but a floor

didn't you go there already   so hard of conditions
that don't come any which way in time

for you having been gone
so given to   so articulated
in the disarrayed c'mon of you

observing the sounds of the world
unboxed   unchaste

if it's the wrong verb   to stay

somewhere in the forward
line of your reactions do you trust

a sensuality less fanciful
ungenetic   plaited
at the service of our obstruction

doesn't it run back too   sending you

this far into this wanting to be about freedom

somebody means the mistakes
hearing two or three birds

in the call of one arching
to visit everywhere onto its name

vaults us to an attitude held   in their soft eyes soft lids
like an end in an image of arches   seeming to open as he passed

Henry emerged singing a hymn of thanksgiving

every night out of "him of thanksgiving"   having gone
again in the typo   in the thing   in which to hide

is how we'll keep leaving it   in the real street
I want to say is the word   and its voice run ahead

to where we can do what we want   not bound even to that

the nation wanes   I'm not afraid you'll turn back

NOTES

The Arabic graffiti appearing across the copyright page can be translated as "Homeland is racist." It is adapted with permission from the digital image "Homeland is racist," 2015, a documentation of a broadcast media hack performed by the Arabian Street Artists (Heba Amin and collaborators). The production company for the TV program *Homeland* sought "Arabian street artists" who might lend a sense of authenticity to its set of a Syrian refugee camp. The artists' intervention aired on October 11, 2015, *Homeland* Season 5, Episode 2.

"Anguish exists. / Man uses his old disasters like a mirror" are the first lines of Roque Dalton's "Ars Poetica" (trans. Hardie St. Martin). I take this book's epigraph from the poem's last line.

A Daughter Having Been of the Type

The term "pledge of resistance" refers to an organizing model popularized by groups seeking to prevent all-out U.S. military intervention in Nicaragua and El Salvador in the 1980s.

Sojourner Truth staged her portrait in the manner of white bourgeois femininity and had it printed as a carte de visite, a photographic calling card, captioned with the statement "I sell the shadow to support the substance," a nod to, among other things, her practice of capitalizing on the sale of these prints to fund her speaking tours.

I borrow and tweak the line "Ellington was only after your confidence" from Fred Moten's *In the Break: The Aesthetics of the Black Radical Tradition*. Moten is quoting Herb Jeffries, a Duke Ellington vocalist, who suggests the listener's ear is an element of a composition waiting to be arranged.

In the Gospel according to John, "glory" gives an arrangement that is self-evident, as when Jesus pulls Lazarus out of his grave. The synoptic Gospels offer instead a Jesus who minds the dynamic between his miracles and what Jews in disparate communities say of his provenance and purpose, often asking some variation of the question, "Who do the people say I am?"

Lists such as "Sacramento then unspecified . . ." refer to sites of executions and lynchings compiled by Ken Gonzales-Day for his book *Lynching in the West: 1850–1935*. His totals by perceived race, nationality, or ethnicity: 8 African Americans, 41 American Indians, 29 Chinese (excluding those shot in the 1871 massacre), 120 Anglo-Americans or persons of European descent, 132 Latin American or Mexican, 22 unknown.

If antiblackness occupies a foundational space in creating the orders that hold out a promise of their breaking, I don't think these tallies trouble that space. I do think they testify to the opportunistic and circumstantial articulations of whiteness as a claim to life.

Rendering his memory of Juan Flores, white vigilante Horace Bell writes: "His eyes, neither black, gray, nor blue, greatly resembling those of the owl—always moving, watchful and wary, and the most cruel and vindictive-looking eyes that were ever set in the human head."

Sepulveda, a major thoroughfare in modern-day Los Angeles, was also the name of the ranch owned by Don Sepulveda where the Barton posse rested on their way to Flores and his men.

Ken Gonzales-Day extracts the definition of the "shout pouch" from period accounts. Reacting to Sheriff Barton's murder, vigilantes lengthened their shout pouches with each kill of a brown man.

A Daughter the Real Horse

I am indebted to Daphne Brooks for her book *Bodies in Dissent: Spectacular Performances of Race and Freedom, 1850–1910*, from which I take the quoted text in this poem. Some of these statements Adah Menken made in letters and in interviews, others come from reviews of her performances written by white male critics.

Making and breaking relations, contexts, and contiguities, Plato's Glaucon waves a mirror about the streets of an imagined city.

"But I reckon I got to light out for the Territory ahead of the rest . . ."—Huck Finn.

Installed on immense spools, panoramas scrolled past the audience offering continuous scenery as if viewed from a galloping horse, a passing boat, or a moving train.

The panorama poem "like reaching running toward . . ." uses and alters phrases from Daphne Brooks's *Bodies in Dissent* and Elin Diamond's *Unmaking Mimesis: Essays on Feminism and Theater*.

"Mr. Hands" was the name Kenneth Pinyan used for himself in the zoophilic community.

"Shake that bear" references a viral video depicting the killing of an adolescent bear, after which the woman who pulls the trigger and her hunting guide enjoy intercourse over the bear's corpse.

"Far be it from me to criticize, but . . ." yields the derogatory labels "farbee" and "farb," applied to U.S. Civil War reenactors who fail to mind the details of their gear, thus jeopardizing their fellows' access to "period ecstasy."

Parian porcelain was developed around 1845 as an inexpensive imitation of marble.

A Daughter That She May Touch the Deployments

In her narrative Sojourner Truth alludes to sexual assault she experienced at a young age at the hands of either Sally or Elizabeth Dumont.

See the poem "Do any black children grow up casual?" by Harmony Holiday.

Retablos in Mexican folk art depict divine interventions into human acts and are often captioned with brief narratives and moral lessons.

"Nobody / no time" is an excerpt from "Nobody," Bert Williams's signature song.

See the poem "The Eye-Beaters" by James Dickey.

I take the lines "A New Rule in Algebra . . ." from a political cartoon published in U.S. newspapers during the Mexican–American War.

See the poem "Beyond My Door, Behind My Back Porch" by Susan Briante.

See a posting by the writer Anne Boyer on, I believe, Instagram.

See the poem "1992" by Alice Notley.

No Address

As a volunteer with International Solidarity Movement, Rachel Corrie practiced the strategy of creating human shields in which activists place themselves among vulnerable populations hoping fear of "first world" state retribution will keep conflicts from escalating into violence. This logic offers bodies with Anglo phenotypes as signs of privileged national status. Other such groups include Witness for Peace and Peace Brigades International.

I take the epigraph "Reportless Subjects . . ." from the poem numbered 1048 in the Thomas H. Johnson edition of *The Complete Poems of Emily Dickinson*.

"[L]et's make like a girl mean something amazing commercial" refers to ads sponsored by the Procter & Gamble conglomerate's Always brand that aim to increase self-confidence in girls entering puberty. P&G's sourcing, research and development, and labor practices have been linked to deforestation, animal abuse, illegal expansion of genetically modified organisms into "third world" markets, and abusive working conditions in migrant-staffed citrus farms in Florida.

"[T]he voice said to Duriel . . ." refers to an incident the poet, composer, and performer Duriel E. Harris shared in a conference talk.

I take the line "a bigger more respectable more competent" from Vladimir Nabokov's *Pale Fire*.

The *Los Angeles Times* reports Predator drone operators flying missions in Afghanistan said, "We see shadows . . ."

"Sleep terrors are episodes of screaming, intense fear and flailing while still asleep." — Mayo Clinic.

Guanshiyin is a female deity to some and a spiritually enlightened human to others. Her name may be translated as "observing the sounds of the world" or "the one who hears the cries of the world." Ceramic figurines depicting Guanshiyin are sometimes cast with a detachable left hand, which petitioners withhold until their prayers are answered. My mother kept one such figurine across our migration.

Part of the nineteenth-century spiritualist movement, spirit dancers summoned multiple male and female spirits of various ethnicities and races in rapid succession while their bodies were committed to the demands of dance.

"Embracing, the dumb will speak, the lame will walk!" is from César Vallejo's poem "Hymn to the Volunteers of the Republic" (trans. James Higgins).

Long Range Acoustic Devices transmit sound at up to 149 decibels, causing immediate head-aches, vertigo, and, in some cases, irreversible hearing loss. The Active Denial System developed by Raytheon projects "a focused millimeter wave energy beam" that produces intolerable heating sensations on skin.

I'm grateful again to Fred Moten, who in helping me think about being a daughter's father used the phrase "the sheer c'mon of her."

In *The Fire Next Time* James Baldwin argues for a sensuality that is "much simpler and much less fanciful" than the simultaneously excessive and diminished sensuality coded by the white racial imaginary into nonwhite bodies.

In *Henry "Box" Brown's Mirror of Slavery*, Brown emerged from the box singing a hymn of thanksgiving, his translation of Psalm 40's lamentation into a song of near-ecstatic pleasure. "[H]im of thanksgiving" is a typo in the song's title as reproduced in the British edition of Brown's *Narrative of the Life of Henry Box Brown, Written by Himself*.

After Brown's production closed, he resurfaced in 1864 walking the streets of Wales dressed as an African king and accompanied by a footman. He appears in the historical record again in 1875 in New England as a magician, blindfolded seer, and spiritualist entertainer by the name of Professor H. Box Brown.

See also reservoir, friend, figure, mirror, obstruction, horse:

Heba Y. Amin, hebaamin.com

Plato's *Phaedrus*

Ange Mlinko's "How Poems Think: The Power of Lyric Poetry Lies in Negation, Not Self-Assertion" in *The Nation*

Dawn Lundy Martin's *Life in a Box Is a Pretty Life*

Adrian Heathfield and Tehching Hsieh's *Out of Now: The Lifeworks of Tehching Hsieh*

Unidentified photographer, *La Chola Martina*, Specialized Libraries and Archival Collections, University of Southern California, reprinted in Ken Gonzales-Day's *Lynching in the West* as plate 12

Barbara McCandless's "The Portrait Studio and the Celebrity: Promoting the Art" in *Photography in Nineteenth Century America*, edited by Martha A. Sandweiss

Mary Niall Mitchell's "'Rosebloom and Pure White,' or So It Seemed" in *American Quarterly*

Terry Carter's documentary film *A Duke Named Ellington*

Sheila E.'s *Romance 1600*

Ilona Katzew's *Casta Painting: Images of Race in Eighteenth-Century Mexico*

Horace Bell's *Reminiscences of a Ranger*

Gustavo Arellano's *OC Weekly* articles "The Assassination of Sheriff James Barton by the Mexican Juan Flores" and "Top 5 Latinas in Orange County History!"

Prince's *Sign o' the Times*

Philip Zarrilly's *The Kathakali Complex: Actor, Performance, and Structure*

Robert Allen's *Horrible Prettiness: Burlesque and American Culture*

International Panorama Council, panoramacouncil.org

John Wieners's *A Superficial Estimation*

Charles Mudede and Robinson

Devor's *Zoo*, a documentary film exploring the life and death of Kenneth Pinyan

Jennifer Christine Nash's *The Black Body in Ecstasy: Reading Race, Reading Pornography*

Allison Smith, allisonsmithstudio.com

The Color of Life: Polychromy in Sculpture from Antiquity to the Present, edited by Roberta Panzanelli, Eike Schmidt, and Kenneth Lapatin

Narrative of Sojourner Truth, a Northern Slave, Emancipated from Bodily Servitude by the State of New York, in 1828

Nell Irvin Painter's *Sojourner Truth: A Life, a Symbol*

Harmony Holiday's *Go Find Your Father / A Famous Blues* and *Hollywood Forever*

The James Dickey Reader, edited by Henry Hart

Susan Briante's *Pioneers in the Study of Motion*

Lindon W. Barrett's *Blackness and Value: Seeing Double*

Bhanu Kapil's *Ban en Banlieue*

Anne Boyer's *Garments Against Women*

Alice Notley's *Grave of Light: New and Selected Poems, 1970–2005*

Predator drone operator transcripts at latimes.com

Cristina Demaria's "The Performative Body of Marina Abramović" in *European Journal of Women's Studies*

Matthew Akers's documentary film *Marina Abramović: The Artist Is Present*

Reverend Hiram Mattison's *Spirit-Rapping Unveiled!*

Jennifer DeVere Brody's *Impossible Purities: Blackness, Femininity, and Victorian Culture*

Tu Fu's *Travels of a Chinese Poet* (trans. Florence Ayscough)

Susan Howe's 1979 interview with Bernadette Mayer for Pacifica Radio

Human Rights Watch, hrw.org

Rachel Corrie Foundation for Peace & Justice, rachelcorriefoundation.org

Aracelis Girmay's *The Black Maria*

Lisa Robertson's *Nilling*

Fred Moten's lecture "Blackness and Nonperformance," available on YouTube

Jeffrey Ruggles's *The Unboxing of Henry Brown*

Tyehimba Jess's *Olio*

Hollis Robbins's "Fugitive Mail: The Deliverance of Henry 'Box' Brown and Antebellum Postal Politics" in *American Studies*

Joanna Brooks's *American Lazarus: Religion and the Rise of African-American and Native American Literatures*

Narrative of the Life of Henry Box Brown, Written by Himself

ACKNOWLEDGMENTS

Earlier versions of some of these poems appeared in the chapbook *My Daughter La Chola* (Ahsahta Press, 2013); in the anthologies *Angels of the Americlypse: An Anthology of New Latin@ Writing* (Counterpath Press, 2014), *Best American Experimental Writing* (Omnidawn Publishing, 2014), *The &Now Awards: The Best Innovative Writing*, volume 3 (Lake Forest College Press, 2014), *Extraordinary Rendition: (American) Writers Speak on Palestine* (OR Books, 2015), and *Resist Much / Obey Little: Inaugural Poems to the Resistance* (Spuyten Duyvil / Dispatches Editions, 2017); in the journals *Black Warrior Review, The Baffler, Bright Pink Mosquito, Cream City Review, Critical Quarterly* (UK), *Denver Quarterly, Huizache: The Magazine of Latino Literature, The Iowa Review, Mandorla: New Writing from the Americas / Nueva Escritura de las Américas, Mizna, Sonora Review, Poetry, Poem: International English Language Quarterly* (UK), *Sous les Pavés, Third Coast, White Wall Review* (Canada); and online at the Dusie Kollectiv's *Tuesday Poem, ESQUE, ONandOnScreen, /One/ The Journal of Literature, Art, and Ideas, past simple*, the Poetry Foundation's *Poem of the Day*, Poets.org, and *Tupelo Quarterly*. Thank you to the curators, editors, and publishers of these spaces.

This work was made possible in part with the support of Headlands Center for the Arts, which afforded me the space and time to begin these poems and then invested a New Works Grant and a second studio residency in their completion. I am deeply grateful to the center's staff and board and to the artists and writers who shared this special place with me.

Thank you to my colleagues and students in the Department of English and in the MFA program at the University of Arizona for their example and encouragement.

This work developed in conversations, some in passing and some intense, with Sam Ace, Rosa Alcalá, Brian Blanchfield, Susan Briante, C. A. Conrad, Hector Corante, Pamela Corante, Tonya

Foster, C. S. Giscombe, Kate Greenstreet, Max Greenstreet, Kimiko Hahn, Duriel E. Harris, Jen Hofer, Harmony Holiday, Janet Holmes, Fady Joudah, Bhanu Kapil, Marcia Klotz, Ruth Ellen Kocher, Paul Laska, Evan Lavender-Smith, Rachel Levitsky, Chris Martin, Dawn Lundy Martin, Leerom Medovoi, Christopher Patrick Miller, Fred Moten, Chris Nealon, Hoa Nguyen, Phil Pardi, Miguel Angel Ramirez, Seph Rodney, Jeff Sirkin, Brandon Shimoda, Allison Smith, Carmen Giménez Smith, Dale Smith, Robert Yerachmiel Snyderman, Juliana Spahr, Ola Stahl, T. C. Tolbert, Divya Victor, Lisa Wells, Ronaldo V. Wilson, and Joshua Marie Wilkinson.

I am grateful to the organizers of the conferences Thinking Its Presence: Race and Creative Writing (University of Montana), Crosstalk, Color and Composition (University of California, Berkeley), and Radius of Arab-American Writers, and I am grateful as well to the curators of the reading series Edge, Intermezzo, and Fair Weather in Tucson, Arizona, Emory Poetry Council at Emory University, Fort Gondo in St. Louis, Missouri, the MFA programs at Boise State University and Mills College, Diesel Books in Oakland, and the Department of English at Johns Hopkins University, where some of these conversations occurred and where I presented this work in progress.

Thank you again to Lindon W. Barrett (1961–2008), who held a space where I could unperform. I should only say he's gone and we are fewer, if we let ourselves be.

Most of all, all gratitude in being with Susan Briante and a daughter who wasn't sent across our lines to be ours.

ABOUT THE AUTHOR

Born in Lima, Peru, to a Syrian mother and Peruvian father, **Farid Matuk** has lived in the United States since the age of six as an undocumented person, a "legal" resident, and a patriated citizen. He is the author of *This Isa Nice Neighborhood* (Letter Machine Editions) and of the chapbooks *My Daughter La Chola* (Ahsahta) and *from Don't Call It Reginald Denny* (Society Editions).